Get Out Of The Boat And Start…
Following Your Dreams

Tony Baker

Printed in the United States of America
ISBN 978-0-9763121-3-0

Disclaimer:
Although the author and publisher have made every effort to ensure that the information in this book was correct at press time, the author and publisher do not assume and hereby disclaim any liability to any party for any loss, damage, or disruption caused by errors or omissions, whether such errors or omissions result from negligence, accident, or any other cause.

This book is not intended as a substitute for the medical advice of physicians. The reader should regularly consult a physician in matters relating to his/her health in particularly with respect to any symptoms that may require diagnosis or medical attention.

DEDICATION

I would like to dedicate this book to Mary "Ma" Barker and Sister Betty Boykin. They were two wonderful, god-fearing women that I love and still miss.

SPECIAL ACKNOWLEDGEMENT

To my uncles Lamar Ricardo Jones and Ellis Albert Jones whom I honor with this book; I love and miss you both.

TO THE READERS

Life is much too short and time is too precious. With that said, thank you so much for investing in me by purchasing this book. May you succeed and achieve your wildest dreams. You have what it takes!

Table of Contents

Chapter One
About the Author

Tony Baker has a combined 20 year career as a life coach, speaker, minister, writer, counselor, and motivator. He holds a Bachelor's degree in Sociology and Master's degree in Psychological Studies.

Tony hosted his own radio talk show which dealt with real life challenges faced by today's youth, families, and communities. He is sought after by educators, businesses, churches, mental health professionals and parents to speak about these issues.

He is a national conference speaker and has travelled throughout the region sharing his message of hope and empowerment. Tony knows how to connect with people while delivering an entertaining, relevant, and inspiring message.

In addition, Tony is listed on the National Speaker's Bureau of the Florida and International Association of Christian Schools and Colleges. He is also a 5-Star Rated Speaker with Thumbtack.com

For more information about Tony or to invite him to speak at your next event, email info@tonybaker.org or visit www.tonybaker.org.

"Your greatest failure is often the commencement of your biggest success."

Tony Baker

Chapter Two

The Declaration of Empowerment

The truth about how I created the affirmation is interesting. During the time when I wrote it, I was going through one of the worst times of my life.

I was having problems in my marriage. After being with the same woman for nearly 25 years, we were contemplating a split. We could not even be in the same room without arguing.

My children were having a rough time as well. The four of them were underperforming and barely passing their classes in school. My wife and I would spend hours helping them study, only for them to bomb on their exams as a result.

At the time, I was working as a Substance Abuse Counselor. The job was very stressful. My direct manager seemed to have it out for me. She was very critical and undermined everyone. To top it all off, we only had 30 minute lunch breaks and had to clock in and out on a time card. Not to mention the daily meetings, two to three large groups every day, and individual sessions to conduct. All of this was done for a very meager salary and without the chance of a raise.

I was also dealing with some personal crises of my own. I had some health challenges. Couple this with the fact that in my mid-40s I was struggling to make it. I had nothing of lasting significance to show for my life. In short, I felt like a failure and was deeply depressed.

One autumn afternoon, I went for a drive after work. After wandering around the area, I stopped in an office parking lot. I sat there in my car for about 30 minutes crying. My shirt was soaked, my eyes were blood shot red, and my nose was running. I picked up my phone and started flipping through it while hoping to find someone I could talk to.

My phone dropped. When I picked it up the "Note" section of my iPhone 4 was open. It was there that I saw this quote that I had written:

"Death and Life is in the power of the tongue..."

I sat and contemplated what that really meant. I had seen and heard that line many times before but this day it took on a greater significance. As I examined the affairs of my life, I recognized that I was speaking more about death than life.

What really held me captive was the portion of the verse that stated, *"In the power of the tongue,"* my tongue. Not anyone else's, but mine. My prospective instantly changed. I began to see how my negative self-talk and defeatist attitude played a part in creating what I was receiving.

It was then that my thoughts began to flow and I penned these words...

Death and Life
Is in the power of my tongue
I will speak words
That edify, build up, motivate, encourage, and bring me closer to my destiny

I speak life
Over my body, over my life, over my family
Over children, over my situations, over my finances

I speak death
To destructive behavior, disease, lack, poverty, and low self-esteem

I believe
That all things are possible

I believe
That if I stay faithful and connected to my higher power
I will have whatever I say

My words shape my world
And nobody can hold me back, but me

I forgive myself, and forgive others
I am healed, I am free, I am special, I am unique,
I am an original masterpiece
Created in the image of God

I speak this and believe it

After I wrote this I began to recite it and my spirit was lifted. The burden I felt was replaced by a sense of empowerment.

As a matter of fact, for the next three weeks I made this my personal declaration. I would say this aloud in my office every morning before I began work. I took it one step further and even placed a copy of the declaration on my wall. Soon afterwards, I was reciting the declaration two to three times per day.

Now let me be transparent. My circumstances did not change, but I began to change in the midst of my circumstances. My marriage got better not because of my wife, but because my prospective changed. I felt more energetic and a greater sense of purpose. After experimenting with the power of the newfound affirmation on myself, I decided to try it out on my large group at work.

These individuals were heavy drug users who had been in and out of many drug rehab facilities and jail. Over 90% of them had substance abuse and co-occurring mental health disorders with suicidal tendencies. There were also a few military veterans diagnosed with Post Traumatic Stress Disorder. Along with this, many of the individuals were also HIV/AIDS positive. In short, these were hardcore people with shattered lives and major problems.

Towards the end of my session I had all of the participants to stand and repeat the affirmation.

As they repeated the affirmation, many of them began to cry. It was as if they were free from their burdens. Those that were unresponsive during the group seemed to come alive. Everyone who repeated the affirmation seemed more energized and encouraged. Just about everyone in the group asked for a copy.

That same week I did the large group once more. I was about to end the session when one of the attendees raised their hand and said,

"Hey Mr. Tony, can we say that thing we said the other day? I really felt better afterwards."

The rest of the group also made similar statements. From that day forward, whenever I ended my large group sessions I would ask the participants to stand and repeat the affirmation aloud.

It became so popular that even staff members would come into my sessions just to recite the affirmation. Many of the staff members also asked me for a copy.

Patients that were being discharged would request a copy to take with them to assist with their sobriety as well as to share it with their family and friends.

I also observed during free time that individuals would form their own groups and read the affirmation together during Bible study, gender groups, or empowerment meetings.

After seeing the results of the affirmation, I began to use it during speaking engagements. Once again, I would get rave reviews and requests for a copy of the affirmation.

Repeated reactions such as this gave me the assurance that others could benefit from this affirmation. As a result of this, I decided to create a book to help people overcome their challenges and live their dreams.

Here are just a few steps that I've found to be helpful in creating the best results when reciting the affirmation:

◊ Read it aloud.
◊ State it with power and conviction.
◊ Recite it with a group for greater intensity. It can also be your family's affirmation/prayer.
◊ Say it by yourself while looking into a mirror. You will be amazed at the impact.
◊ For greater results, read it three times a day; morning, noon, and before bedtime.

"To wait on conditions and circumstances to change before you live your dreams is like watching paint dry."
Tony Baker

Chapter Three

Give me my dreams or give me death

"YOU CAN ASK FOR ANYTHING IN MY NAME, AND I WILL DO IT..."

John 14:14

A politician, planter, attorney and one of America's Founding Fathers, Patrick Henry was a tremendous force during the movement for independence. In spite of his leadership to end the Stamp Act in 1765, he is best remembered for his statement, "...But as for me, give me liberty or give me death..." This is the attitude we need when pursuing our desired outcomes. We must continue through the corridors of dreams with the passion and vigorousness of Patrick Henry.

I asked one of my colleagues, "When do you stop trying to achieve your dreams?" His answer was quick, yet profound as he pointed out, "Until you die."

Death!

That should be the only thing that stops us from attempting to do what we have never done before. Death should be the only obstacle between us and our desires. In my current stage of life I have no other alternative.

I was too impatient to keep one job for 20 to 25 years and retire. So at this point, if you are like me, trying to stay on a job hoping to work for retirement just will not do it. I would have to wait until I am 69 or 74 years old for a retirement check. Frankly, it probably wouldn't cover my desired living expectations.

In short, my dreams are more valuable than retirement. I grew tired of filling out applications online with every job now requiring that you take some type of psychological test. If you don't score well you can't even get a job at a fast food restaurant.

You may be thinking,

"Go back to school and get more education?"

My student loan is more than one of my house notes. No, I don't need more education. I possess a Master's degree.

Now you may say,

"Join a club or auxiliary or become a Mason where you can get more connected?" I thought about it, but there are many who have tried the connection route towards achieving success. Sometimes the price of being connected is too high a price to pay though. No, give me my God and my dreams or give me death…

I often meditate on these thoughts,

"Lord I don't want to die in my reality…Let me live to see my dreams not in 20 years, not in 15 years, not even 1 year… But right now! Let me walk in the fulfillment of your promises. Oh Father, let me bask in the commencement of my heart's desire. So the question will no longer haunt me… "When Do I Stop Trying to Achieve My Dreams?"

Chapter Four

The ABC's of Motivation

"YOU WILL KNOW YOU ARE A SUCCESS WHEN PEOPLE DON'T HAVE TO ASK WHAT YOU DO BECAUSE THEY'LL KNOW WHAT YOU HAVE DONE"...

Tony Baker

As you pursue your dreams from time to time, you will run into situations that may cause you to become discouraged. In an effort to keep you inspired here are some motivational phrases to lift you up when you feel like a failure. You can also use these phrases to prevent unwanted feelings or to maintain your strategic edge. I call them ABC's of Motivation.

A - Accept yourself for who you are.
B - Believe that you can and you will.
C – Creativity is within you.
D – Don't ever give up or give in.
E – Elevate your thinking.
F – Fight on no matter the odds against you.
G – God will provide where He guides.
H – Hold on to your dreams.

I – Ideas and information are your keys to success.
J – Just be yourself.
K – Kindness can carry you a long way.
L – Learning is a lifelong pursuit.
M – Multiply what is working for you.
N – Never lie, cheat or steal. Always play by the rules.
O – Open up to new possibilities.
P – Patience is needed when trying to achieve your dreams.
Q – Quitters never win and winners never quit.
R – Rest! Even God took a day off.
S – Stop procrastinating.
T – Take control of your destiny.
U – Unity with family and friends is vital.
V – Victory belongs to those who don't vacate their vision.
W – Wisdom is essential to your success.
X – X Factors are the strengths that lie within.
Y – You were born to win.
Z – Zero in on what you really desire.

Chapter Five

The 5 E's To Acceleration

"IF YOU AIM TOO LOW THERE IS NOWHERE TO GO, BUT IF
YOU AIM HIGHER THEN YOU WILL REACH YOUR DESIRE"...

Tony Baker

When I hosted my radio talk show called "The Talking with Tony Show" I interviewed a guy by the name of Alvin Brown. Alvin was the Director of The Willie Gary Classic. The classics were a huge success and helped to raise money for at-risk youth and other projects. Since that time, Alvin Brown has gone on to become the 1st African-American Mayor of the City of Jacksonville, Florida. Even before his history making political career, Alvin embodied the 5 E's To Acceleration.

Energy

Most successful people are able to maintain their energy level. There is a bounce in their step. In successful people, there is a fervent look in their eyes. One way to measure your progress is through your energy level. Low energy leads to low outcomes.

Enthusiasm

Enthusiasm is contagious! You can always tell when a person is on a mission. Their zeal will show. If your enthusiasm represented a fire, how many things would be set on fire?

Empowered

The true visionary is empowered. Another word for empowerment is resourceful. If a dreamer doesn't have it, they find a way to get it. If they don't know it, they learn it. To live your dreams you must be willing to be empowered.

Emotionality

When I speak of emotionality I am talking about being able to balance your emotions. Strong dreamers and visionaries have learned to deal with failures, challenges, and changes without getting flustered.

Expansive

As a pursuer of your dreams, you must learn to live in two worlds. You must live in the now and prepare for the future. This takes expansive thinking. To think in an expansive manner means that you always keep the end result in mind.

Chapter Six
Next Is Not Enough

"ONE GUY SAID "I COULD NEVER DO THAT" AND ANOTHER ONE SAID, "I THINK I COULD DO THAT." THE LAST GUY SAID "I CAN DO THAT." EACH ONE OF THEM IS RIGHT"...

Tony Baker

I never heard anyone say they desired their aspirations to be delayed. In "Next Is Not Enough," I share a story about how standing in a shopping market line gave me a sense of urgency to press towards my dreams.

I was in line awaiting service at a clothing store. The person in front of me had finally gone and I was next.

Although I was next, the person who had just gone before me took forever. They had several receipts, exchanges, and they even argued with the store representative.

While waiting, a thought came to my mind,

"Next is not enough."

I knew I would eventually get my chance to take care of my purchases, but being next just did not seem to have any benefits at the time.

I equated my situation of being next in line to fulfilling my goals, aspirations, and dreams.

Then I thought to myself,

"No, I did not want to be next to live my dreams; I want to live them now."

In baseball, if there are two outs and the next batter strikes out, the individual who was next will not get a chance at bat.

I believe it is the same thing with our desires. We want to be at bat swinging, not hoping to be next.

Have you ever prayed and asked to be next or do you pray and ask to be now?

Today, do not settle for next, but wait if you have to. When it is your turn at bat swing hard and play smart while keeping in the back of your mind...next is not enough!

Chapter Seven
3 Fears That Forfeit Forward Progress

"EVEN THOUGH I WALK THROUGH THE VALLEY OF THE
SHADOW OF DEATH, I WILL FEAR NO EVIL."

Psalm 23:4 NIV

One of the scariest movies I had ever seen (at that time) was
Nightmare on Elm Street. The movie featured Freddy
Kruger who was an undead serial killer. He had the ability
to kill people in their sleep. Because of my intense fear after
seeing this movie, I slept with my mother for over a month.
Fear caused me many sleepless nights at that time. What is
fear costing you? Better still are you fearful of starting that
business, writing that book or achieving those goals.
Whatever the case you should not let fear stop your success.

Fear of Failure
Sometimes even the hint of likely failure can keep a
person from trying to make attempts at a difficult task. This
breakdown is looked upon by them to be crippling both

psychologically and physiologically as they seem to be very fearful to face such a possibility. This could be due to many connecting factors, one of which could be the need to look accomplished and always successful.

Fear of the possibility of experiencing unpleasant or painful outcomes

This too can keep a person from trying innovative things or even getting anything done at all. This could come from a bad experience which the individual has yet to come to terms with. Therefore, they conveniently use this particular excuse as a good way to inject procrastination into the equation. Although this could sometimes be the actual very real and previously experienced issue, using this as an excuse will not help the individual in future endeavors and it will not help build good character elements.

Fear of missing out

For the person who wants to do everything, experience everything and be everything, burning out can quickly turn the individual into a person who sooner or later resorts to putting things off as a defense mechanism. This usually happens for those who have the "go getter and have it all" mindset, which mostly only works to a certain limit until exhaustion and burnout set in.

Chapter Eight

The 7 P's That Will Hinder Your Success

"Never place your dreams in someone else's hand"...
Tony Baker

In 8th grade, I ran the first leg of the 4x100 relay. My coach would always say, "When you come out of the starting blocks keep your head down and focus on running in your lane...never look around to see what the other runners are doing because it will slow you down." Are you keeping your head down while focusing on your dreams and aspirations? Or, are you too busy worrying about what others are doing? You can't run your race and stare at others at the same time. This will hinder you from finishing strong. With that said, here are the 7 P's that often hinder individuals' success.

Past

There is a quote from a movie that says, "You might be done with your past, but your past is not done with you." Don't allow an earlier period of past problems to prevent you from progressing. The only people that don't make mistakes are 6 feet underground.

People

Take a good look at the people around you. Now here is a powerful prospective. You are only as rich, strong, and influential as the four closet people in your life. If those four people are broke, weak, and lack influence, then soon you will be the fifth.

Pity (Self)

Wallowing in self-pity never breeds achievement. Anyone who is trying to improve their life is going to run into a wall or two. Give yourself eight hours to deal with "it." Afterwards, have a funeral for "it" and get on with your life. Besides, most people have too many problems of their own. They don't really have time for yours.

Pessimist

If you are prone to pessimism it will be an uphill battle for you to master yourself and improve your life. The central reason is because you have to be your own best friend, encourager, and advocate. Pessimists are often their own worst enemy.

Pressure

Anxious self-talk leads to doubt, fear, and lack of progress. When confronting a situation that can causes pressure, keep this in mind. There is always someone, somewhere that has either been through what you are going through or had a similar experience. Their triumph over the issue should provide you with the hope you need to accomplish your goals.

Prejudice

Prejudice can be broken down into two words, "Pre (before) and Judice (Judge)." To be prejudice means to prejudge someone. The root emotion attached to prejudice is pride. One ancient proverb says, "Pride precedes a disaster, and an arrogant attitude precedes a fall." Every bird in the air has to one day come down. They either land or they are shot down. If you continue operating with a prejudice spirit then the latter will be your downfall.

Procrastination

Procrastinators masquerade in fear. I believe they do so because they have a fear of failure. It easy to keep putting off pursuing your dreams by saying, "I am still planning," "The time is not right," "I just want to be sure," or even "This might not be God's Will." Well, I can tell you one thing. The results you can have are those that imminent from action. No action, no results, no advancement.

"The fastest runner doesn't always win the race, and the strongest warrior doesn't always win the battle. The wise sometimes go hungry, and the skilful are not necessarily wealthy. And those who are educated don't always lead successful lives. It is all decided by chance, by being in the right place at the right time."
Ecclesiastes 9:11 NLT

Chapter Nine

The Nudge

"NOW TO HIM WHO IS ABLE TO DO EXCEEDINGLY
ABUNDANTLY ABOVE ALL THAT WE ASK OR THINK,
ACCORDING TO THE POWER THAT WORKS IN US..."

Ephesians 3:20

When I was out of town conducting training sessions I called my wife to tell her goodnight before I went to bed. After speaking with her, I hung up the phone. I had laid down for about 10 minutes when something inside of me said, "Call your wife. She left the front door unlocked." I ignored it initially and tried to lie back down. However, this time the voice inside me was even louder, "Call your wife and tell her that the front door is unlocked." So I gave in and called. I explained to her what had taken place and then hung up the phone. A minute later she called back and said, "Wow! You were right...the front door was unlocked." That was one example of The Nudge.

Have you ever sat around and thought to yourself,

"I could be doing more..."

"I should be living better."

"I should be further along."

Now here is the cold hard truth....You should be! (And so should I)

You are absolutely right to be upset with yourself. (And so should I)

Now here is the good news. I believe those feelings inside you are from God to push you forward.

I call it "The Nudge" from the All-Knowing.

One definition of nudge is *to prod (someone) gently, typically with one's elbow, in order to draw their attention to something.*

The Nudge is also designed to kill the killer of dreams, which is complacency.

Those desires in your heart will be granted.

This is especially true if those Nudges have been strong and unrelenting.

God does not want you to give up on your goals.

I believe this is true because he placed those dreams in your heart.

However, God cannot grant what you have given up.

You must hang in there and stay tenacious until your time.

Let me be very transparent and say this, *"It can feel at times that God is playing a dirty trick on you in terms of achieving your dreams."*

It can sometimes feel like the world is succeeding, but you are stagnant.

However, if the Nudge is still knocking then it means that those dreams are coming closer.

Whatever you do, keep fighting for your future and listen to...

The Nudge of the All-Knowing...

Chapter Ten
1,009

"GOD HAS NO SKIP PLAN, YOU MUST WAIT IN LINE LIKE EVERYONE ELSE"...

Tony Baker

If reaching goals were easy then everyone would be rich, famous, and healthy. The fact is, trying to accomplish anything worthwhile can be a task. What can be even worse is trying and continuously failing. For most people that is the case. However, you will see a different scenario in 1,009.

So you have this chicken recipe. This new flavor is supposed to be really good. At least it is good to you.

But wait a moment.

How old are you?

You mean to tell me at this age, this stage in life, you want to start a business?

Well, at nearly 70 years old one man did just that. He did it using only his social security check.

After 1,008 tries, on the 1,009th try Colonel Sanders finally found someone to believe in him and Kentucky Fried Chicken was born.

Even after 1,008 tries, he kept knocking.

When did you stop knocking for opportunities?

Was it after the 5th rejection? No, perhaps it was the 103rd failure.

After 1,008 attempts, Colonel Sanders found someone to believe in him.

I believe the real thing he discovered was, "Never stopped believing in yourself."

Neither should you stop believing. Keep Dreaming!

Chapter Eleven
You Already Are!

"EVERY DREAM HAS TWO THINGS IN COMMON... A START
POINT AND END POINT. EVERYTHING IN BETWEEN IS THE
RIDE"...

Tony Baker

The journey to success takes many turns. There may be times
where it seems as if your best efforts just aren't good
enough. It can also feel as if you are carrying the weight of
the world on your shoulders while others are carrying a
feather. I hope this next narrative gives you hope for the
journey.

I remember when the following was happening in my life:
- I had been unemployed for 2 ½ years
- My lights had been turned off because I couldn't pay
  the bill
- I would get up at night to ride around in my car, so
  that the repo man would not take it
- I had no food in my house to feed my family
- I was depressed and on the verge of collapse

I finally went to a payday loan place to take out one of those crazy loans with the ridiculous interest rate in order to get my lights turned on and food in the house.

While waiting in line at the grocery store, I looked up to heaven with tears running down my face and said,

"God, make me into a winner."

God looked down from heaven and said,

"I can't make you something that <u>you already are.</u>"

No matter your current circumstance, situation, or dilemma, you are a winner and you will succeed at life because...You Already Are!

Chapter Twelve

Finish What You Start!

"IF YOU ARE ALLERGIC TO PROBLEMS THEN YOU CAN'T TAKE
THE MEDICATION OF SUCCESS"...

Tony Baker

I started my Master's program in 2003. There was a comprehensive exam that I had to pass in order to receive my degree. I failed the exam 12 times. Finally in December of 2008, I passed the exam and received my Master's degree. Failure, setbacks, and challenges will always come. However, you have to make it your goal to finish what you start.

Finish what you start! One famous saying goes, "The race is not given to the swift, neither the battle to the strong, nor bread to the wise, but it is given to the one that endures until the end."

I know this has been a rough year with its economic woes, relationship problems, and countless other burdens that you carry.

However, I believe in you and know that you have what it takes to move forward.

Make up your mind right now to finish what you start.

Bill Gates didn't quit when Microsoft failed. Its initial name was Traf-O-Data.

Oprah was abused as a child, fired, and told she wasn't fit for television.

Moses was called to lead a multitude of people, but had a speech impediment.

My point is simple. All of these people and many others started, but did not quit.

Finish what you start!

Chapter Thirteen
The One Thing You Should Never Rely On

"LIVING YOUR DREAMS IS A MINUTE BY MINUTE PROCESS, NOT AN OVERNIGHT SUCCESS"...

Tony Baker

I can remember one beautiful, sunny morning waking up to hear the weather report: "There is a 90% chance of rain." I said to myself, "Yea right." About 2PM that afternoon, while walking in the mall, I heard the thunder boom. When I stepped outside it was pouring rain. I left my umbrella in the car. I could have prayed, screamed, and hollered, but the umbrella could not keep me dry. Although it had the potential to do so; potential has never helped anyone as you will see.

The one thing you should never rely on is what N.F.L. owners & coaches rely on during the Draft...

POTENTIAL!!!

Let me ask you something.

If a person needed healing from cancer, how can potential heal them?

If you were broke and needed money, can potential get you the wealth you are looking for?

No one ever got a promotion by potentially asking for one.

Here are some names. Tell me what they all have in common:

◊   Tim Couch
◊   Brain Bosworth
◊   JaMarcus Russell
◊   Ki-Jana Carter
◊   Archie Griffin

All of these players were drafted in the first round of the N.F.L.

Yet none of them did anything with lasting implications in the N.F.L.

Your potential is only maximized once it is realized and released.

Here is a thought...

"Potential is only powerful when it is fully utilized. Otherwise, **potential is the poison of progress.**"

Chapter Fourteen

The 4 I's To Unfriend Unproductive People

"HE WHO WALKS WITH WISE MEN WILL BE WISE, BUT THE COMPANION OF FOOLS WILL BE DESTROYED."

Proverbs 13:20 NKJV

There are so many tremendous individuals who are destined for greatness, but never grow.

One of the reasons they are not growing is because of the drama in their lives due to unproductive people. Here are four simple steps to overcoming drama so that you can live your dreams.

Insight - Try this experiment now. Take the palm of your hand and put it on your forehead. Now move your palm back so that you can see your entire hand. The people you hang around are like the palm of your hand on your forehead. You can't see the wholeness of that friendship/relationship because they are too close. But when you move your palm back, you are able to see your entire hand. What I'm trying to say is that there may be people in your life that are smothering you. Sometimes the smothering is intentional to prevent you from effectively evaluating your relationship with them. Once you investigate those areas and gain insight, you must take the next step if they are hindering you. You may have to ignore them.

Ignore - Yes, I know it sounds rude but this is the next step. Go ahead and block their number(s). Erase them from your cell phone and unfriend them on Facebook. No more Tweets on Twitter either. You have to move your life in a better direction. You have missed out on too much for too long. Listen to objectivity and wisdom. Trust me, after about two weeks of little to no conversation they will get the message. If not, you may have to let them know that you are going to a place called destiny and only have room for one other person, and God has already taken that seat.

Initiate - Now that you are ignoring the drama, it is time for you to initiate some of the things you really desire to do. Start that book, blog, bank account, or bake sell that you've always wanted to do. You might as well try something you've never tried before. There is no one in your life trying to hold you back. You are going to be amazed at your results. Life will unfold for you since you've gotten rid of the dead weight. This is the experimentation phase of your dream planning. This is the place where you give yourself permission to fail, take calculated risks, and go for the gusto.

Ignite - Once you have initiated your dreams, it is now time for you to streamline your vision. *"Too many irons in the fire can burn the house down"* (That was a Tony Baker original). So try to choose those areas in your life that come naturally. You will begin to discover that certain talents and gifts are inborn. Once you have narrowed down those things you really want to accomplish, go after them! Do something every day that brings you closer to your dreams.

This is how you overcome drama and live you dreams.

"If your success came without a fight, it won't last through the dark nights."
Tony Baker

Chapter Fifteen

The Biggest Mistake Most People Make

"DON'T ALIGN YOURSELF WITH SOMEONE JUST BECAUSE THEY SHARE SIMILAR A VISION. MCDONALD'S AND BURGER KING BOTH SELL HAMBURGERS, BUT THEY BOTH DO IT VERY DIFFERENTLY"...

Tony Baker

Comparing a machete to a gun is not much of a comparison. They both can be used as weapons. On the contrary, a gun in the hands of a novice is no match for an expert machete user. This is why we cannot afford to make one of the biggest mistakes of all.

We have all heard the phrase, *"It is like comparing apples to oranges."*

Both are fruits, but the greatest commonalty is the comparison. We often compare ourselves with one another. We compare:

◊ Our success
◊ The rate of our success
◊ How much money we make

◊   The success of our children
◊   Our looks
◊   The size of our houses
◊   The types of cars we drive

It is easy to compare yourself to others when you have accomplished a great deal more. On the contrary, comparisons can drive you crazy when you have yet to accomplish what you really desire.

One of the reasons why comparisons are an unfair way of measuring success is because of the journey factor. You just never know the journey of someone's life and how they arrived at where they are.

For instance, I know of one ministry leader, who within five years went from one major mega ministry (and I mean huge churches) to another. He is now with one of the largest churches in the world serving as their top minster.

If you were a minister and tried to compare yourself to someone like that, then many questions would enter your mind. You may even become discouraged and think in your heart, "God is not just or fair. What is he doing that I am not? They must be really special and far more talented than me."

The point I am making is this, "Don't compare yourself to others but measure by where you are with what you can become."

I leave you with a quick story.

About 17 years ago, Microsoft was predicted to corner the market with their online product Magna Carta Encyclopedia. Around the same time, a group of volunteers banded together to start a similar concept in terms of dispensing information through encyclopedias online.

Today, Microsoft's online Magna Carta Encyclopedia is almost non-existence. However, the group of individuals who band together now has the world's most used online encyclopedia.

The name of the group is...Wikipedia.

If you would have compared Microsoft's Magna Carta to Wikipedia back then, most people would have chosen the Microsoft product without a doubt.

This is why you should give yourself a break and stop comparing yourself with others. You never know what God has in store. Just ask Wikipedia.

"If everything is perfect in your life, check your pulse and make sure your heart is beating."
Tony Baker

Chapter Sixteen

7 Days

"IT NEVER MATTERS HOW MANY PEOPLE ARE FOR OR
AGAINST YOU. YOU PLUS GOD IS ALWAYS THE MAJORITY"...
Tony Baker

What do you call an 86-year-old woman with the energy of a
20-year-old? The spirit and zest for the life like a teenager.
She has a heart of gold, the class of a first lady, and to top it
all off she wears stilettos every day -- we call her Ma Barker.
Mary Barker is the hero of many people in her town, and
certainly was at our previous church.

Recently, she had some health problems. The doctors
told her that she had some form of stomach cancer. She lay
in that hospital bed for a couple weeks. The doctors told her
that they had to operate to remove the cancer. In typical Ma'
Barker fashion she refused the procedure.

As a matter of fact the last thing she would ever do was
take a bunch of medication, let alone allow doctors to
perform a major surgery on her.

They gave her 7 days to live. Tears flooded the eyes of
many people as the news spread. Seven days is what the

doctors said. Well, the doctors did not know Ma' Barker, her faith, or the God she served.

I am glad to report that she out lived the doctor's predictions. Since then, she has gone on to be with her Maker.

However, the morale of the story is this. Doctors may know science, but it is best that you know your God. If you don't, you may very well take your last breath in 7 days, or your seventh day could become the string of many more pleasant times.

Chapter Seventeen
Traffic Signs to Success

"IF YOU ARE WAITING FOR THE RAIN AND SNOW TO STOP,
YOU WILL NEVER START DOWN THE ROAD TO SUCCESS"...
Tony Baker

See how many traffic signals you recognize. Email me your results at: info@tonybaker.org

There's Only One Way To Go
But there are many Dead Ends
There will also be Detours, Flashing Lights and even Road Blocks with Workers Present
You may even have to drive over Potholes
As you pursue your dreams you may come to a Fork in the Road
You will have to turn Left or Right
If you go the Wrong Way
Just remember to make a U-Turn
Whatever you do
Don't Park in Procrastination
Never Yield to quitting
Do Not Enter into giving up

Sometimes you must Slow Down and Proceed with Caution
It may feel like you are going slower than driving through a School Zone
Don't lose heart, just Buckle Up because it's The Law and God's will for you to achieve
And remember to Share the Road to success
Go for what you believe in
Ride with the Traffic of champions and Give Way to God
There is always Reserved Parking for those who never give up!

Chapter Eighteen

10 Ways to Increase Your Confidence

"SO DO NOT THROW AWAY YOUR CONFIDENCE; IT WILL BE RICHLY REWARDED."

Hebrews 10:35 NIV

The first time I was asked to give a talk to high school students I bombed. I spent the entire speech trying to mimic someone else because I was unsure of my own ability. I learned a valuable lesson that day. "You can't be confident in someone that you are not." As you read and apply these keys to confidence, I hope you gain the strength you need to be who you are instead of someone you are not.

◊ Questioning the worse conceivable outcome and accepting that it's not the end of the world.

◊ Trying new things and achieving some level of success. Even if the success is small, it will help to build self-confidence levels instantaneously.

◊ Listening to music that lifts the emotional state and motivates the individual to get the task done swiftly and resourcefully is also another option.

◊ Making plans and sticking to them, even when everyone says it is not feasible, will help to boost both the outcome and your confidence levels.

◊ Using introspection to draw on the inner strengths also helps to boost self-confidence instantly. There are methods where the breathing styles help to cause a chemical reaction within the body to give it that extra boost.

◊ Exercising is also a great self-confidence booster. The chemical reaction within the body allows it to push limits.

◊ Facing fears will also give the individual the inner confidence to overcome challenges.

◊ Creating something that is useful will contribute positively to immediate elevated self-confidence levels.

◊ Realizing that past errors don't dictate the person's capabilities to venture forth is also another form of increasing self-confidence.

◊ Improving social skills will also help the individual to attract more positive attention, thus contributing to raising a person's level of confidence.

Chapter Nineteen

You Must Step Before You See It

IF GOD HAS GIVEN YOU THE VISION TO SEE IT, HE WILL
ALSO GIVE YOU THE POWER TO POSSESS IT"...

Tony Baker

For the most part, in order to get paid on a job you must work. Very few companies will pay individuals for work they have not done. The same applies here. No effort, no results.

Have you noticed that God rarely reveals everything there is to know about a new opportunity, business venture, dream, or destiny?

Maybe this happens because if you knew how things would turn out there would be no need for faith.

Faith is most needed when you are unsure of yourself and the direction you are headed.

When action is required and you are unclear about the effectiveness of the direction you must take, just remember the story of Joshua.

God told Joshua to cross over the Jordan River. But there was no clearance in the waters for him and the people to cross over.

At that point a decision had to be made. Perhaps it is the same decision that you are contemplating, "Do I follow my faith or do I stay in safety?"

I am sure Joshua was nervous and may have felt unsure about his potential outcome, but when the priest stepped into the water, it gave way to them and they crossed over (Joshua 3:14-16).

Your visions and dreams are the same way. When you make up your mind to step into all that God has for you, the things you thought would hinder your progress will start to give way just like the waters did for Joshua and God's Chosen People.

The money, business, and opportunities are well within your grasp. However, I must warn you.

If you are waiting for your circumstances to be perfect, your credit score to get better, the raise to come through, or people to align themselves with you, then you may very well miss crossing over.

Joshua and God's Chosen People were not perfect, but God's ability to make things happen for them was.

So stop worrying and start stepping.

Chapter Twenty

Perspective Acceptance

"IF SOMEONE CAN TALK YOU OUT OF YOUR DREAMS, YOUR EFFORTS WOULD HAVE BEEN A NIGHTMARE"...

Tony Baker

Too often we place more emphasis on what others say about us as opposed to how we view ourselves. Perspective Acceptance was written to shatter that point of view.

There will always be things in life to challenge your perspective.

The great thing is that you don't have to accept what others say.

Don't even allow how someone else feels about you block your progress.

The most important person in the equation is not how others view you, what they say, or how they feel about you...it is how you see yourself and what you tell yourself.

Why?

This is very simple, because you have the privilege of being with yourself 24 hours a day and 7 days a week.

This is one of the reasons you should be your biggest fan and cheerleader.

We all have weaknesses, have made mistakes, and done things we should not have done. Focus on your strengths and keep developing your mind and skill sets.

You are almost there.

Chapter Twenty-One

How to Stay Positive in a Negative World

"NEGATIVITY IS NEEDED TO SHOW THE PRESENCE OF POSITIVITY"...

Tony Baker

The darkest room in the history of mankind cannot extinguish the smallest light. That light will penetrate the depth of any darkness. Operating in a positive spirit in this age is a game changer. Your positive persona will illuminate the darkness of negativity that infiltrates many of our institutions. Besides, if we never see darkness, we could never appreciate the light. Here are a few principles to assist you in maintaining your positive outlook.

◊ Listening to podcasts, CDs and other audio presentations which the main theme is staying optimistic. This helps to create a positive mindset that is equipped to face difficult situations.

◊ Read encouraging and inspiring material frequently. Put up stickers and post ads that have upbeat captions to encourage this positive mindset. Try to spiritually and physically put into practice all that is learned from analyzing such beneficial material.

◊ Staying in good physical shape, keeping a well-balanced diet and an exercise regimen also helps the individual to stay within a positive frame in both body and mind, which transcends into a positive attitude. When all is working well, positivity is the theme of the day.

◊ Understanding and accepting that things don't always go as planned helps the individual to adjust accordingly while still staying optimistic. This is a very important state of mind to have in order to stay upbeat, as almost nothing today is totally predictable at all times.

◊ Surrounding one's self with other encouraging people also helps to stay productive. It would be very unlikely for one person to display negative traits in the presence of a whole group of positively minded individuals. By being in the company of positive people, one would be able to not only emulate this good quality but will also learn to control their negative mindset altogether.

◊ Acknowledging the negativity is often encouraged rather than trying to side step it.

◊ Calling too much attention to it may bring about the realization of its existence.

◊ Present and model positive elements to emulate. This is sometimes more helpful than actually trying to physically or mentally change the situation.

◊ Refrain from making an already negative situation into an even bigger mess.

◊ Using some simple physical exercises, like breathing in deeply, when the onset of any negativity begins.

◊ Focus on the strengths rather than the weaknesses.

Chapter Twenty-Two
15 Ways to Get Rapid Results

"THE PLANS OF THE DILIGENT LEAD TO PROFIT, AS
SURELY AS HASTE LEADS TO POVERTY."

Proverbs 21:5 NIV

The microwave is often used as an analogy when discussing
speed. In the 1940's the microwave oven was discovered by
accident after Engineer Percy Spencer's candy bar melted in
his pocket while standing near a vacuum tube that generates
microwave signals. He experimented with popcorn Kernels
and eggs. Then in 1947 Raytheon patented the dielectric
heating device. He initially called it "The Radarange." It
weighed 800 lbs. and sold for $2000 to $3000 thousand
dollars. Now put into practice these principles to help you
get microwavable, rapid results.

◊   Keep your desktop free of clutter.
◊   Create a space to put papers that you need to
deal with eventually.
◊   Create systems or ways of doing this for your
business.
◊   Outsource tasks that you don't need to
personally do, or don't want to do.

◊   Do business tasks during your business time only.

◊   Be devoted to just one project at a time.

◊   Set boundaries when you answer emails, calls, and others form of communication.

◊   Use the Pomodoro Technique-25 minute intervals to complete tasks.

◊   Schedule closed-door and quiet periods of time.

◊   Do productivity checks.

◊   Don't get lost in multi-tasking.

◊   Always generate a growing sense of optimism.

◊   Create your business around your passion.

◊   Schedule your more challenging work during your prime time.

◊   Incorporate a reward system for a job well done.

Chapter Twenty-Three
When to Distance Yourself from Negative Co-Workers or Friends

"DON'T BE FOOLED BY THOSE WHO SAY SUCH THINGS, FOR "BAD COMPANY CORRUPTS GOOD CHARACTER."
Corinthians 15:33 NLT

I remember when I was in the seventh grade there was this guy who always hung around me. When my mother met him she told me he was nothing but trouble. Being young and gullible, I did not see what she saw. Needless to say she was right. It was confirmed when she bought me a pair tennis shoes. He and I switched shoes during school. After school I went looking for him but he was nowhere to be found.

A week passed and he came to school with my shoes claiming that he bought some that looked just like mine. If I had known the principles I am about to share with you (or just listened to my mother) then I could have avoided the situation altogether. There will be times when you have to distance yourself from certain people on your job. Below are easy and simple methods to help you manage your relationships as you move forward in your career.

◊ If negativity enfolds with that person no matter how hard you tried to inflict positivity onto him.

◊ If the person has nothing in common with you.

◊ If the person is obliging you to listen to his complaints and negativity every day just because he has once stood beside you in your darkest moment.

◊ If the person sends you negative feelings such as anger, depression, frustration, doubt and other negative signals.

◊ If the person is doing something that causes you to dread seeing him again.

Chapter Twenty-Four
How Listening Skills Can Enhance Your Career, Life, and Relationships

"BIG FAT EARS ARE MORE DESIROUS THAN A BIG FAT MOUTH"...

Tony Baker

There is one skill that is often overlooked but is very important. That skill is the ability to listen to others. There will be times when a co-worker, friend, or business associate just needs someone to hear them out. The ability to listen in an empathic manner can assist you in creating a connection that could thrust your career to the next level. Here are some tips on being an effective and empathic listener.

◊ Willingness to let the other parties dominate the discussion.
◊ Paying attention to what is being said.
◊ Caring about not interrupting.
◊ Use of open-ended questions.
◊ Sensitivity to the emotions being expressed.
◊ Ability to reflect back to the other individual, the substance, and feelings being expressed.

Listening attentively encompasses:

◊ Acknowledgement of the speaker.
◊ Increasing the speaker's self-respect and self-confidence.
◊ Telling the speaker, "You're important" and "I'm not judging you."
◊ Gaining the speaker's cooperation.
◊ Decreasing tension and stress.
◊ Establishing teamwork.
◊ Acquiring trust.
◊ Eliciting openness.
◊ Acquiring a sharing of ideas and thoughts.
◊ Obtaining more valid information about the individual and the issue.

➢ Empathic Listening Technique # 1: Allow Others to Control the conversation.
➢ Empathic Listening Technique # 2: Ask Questions.
➢ Empathic Listening Technique # 3: Reflect After Everything.

Chapter Twenty-Five

Determination

"DETERMINATION IS THE DIFFERENCE BETWEEN LIVING YOUR DREAMS VS. LIVING IN DREADFULNESS"...

Tony Baker

Stay determined
Stay bold and you will always make it
Nothing or no one can stop you
Stay the course and you'll go through
Failure is not failure. It is only a state of mind
Outcomes and results are the only things that last
Just look how far you've come
You have gone through worst in the past
Shake off all of your challenges
Move the doubt aside
Maintain strong determination and walk with pride
Trouble doesn't last long
Your strength will outlast
Soon and very soon,
This too shall pass...

"Opportunities are always knocking, if you are willing to open new doors."
Tony Baker

Chapter Twenty-Six

Are you more afraid of dying or not living your destiny?

"CEMETERIES ARE FILLED WITH PEOPLE WHO FAILED TO COMPLETE GOD'S BEST PLAN FOR THEIR LIVES"...

Tony Baker

We all must die out of life. There is no other way. Therefore, it is critical that we stay the course and accomplish as much as we can while we have strength in our bodies and air in our lungs. As I mentioned before, death is inevitable. Since that is the case, why can't accomplishing our dreams be inevitable as well?

You only die once, but your destiny can occur at any moment.

Let me ask you something...

If you were to die today, do you think you would have completed what you have been placed on earth to accomplish?

Destiny can be defined "as the predetermined, usually inevitable or irresistible, course of events."

I believe what trips us up is the word "predetermined." I think of predetermined as being the highest intention of what should happen, but hasn't yet. If you think on those lines it is easy to see how a person could have good outcomes, but not experience their best predetermined plan. Here are a few examples:

◊ Abraham and Sarah were supposed to only have Isaac, but they also had Ismael who became a thorn in the inside of the Children of Israel.

◊ The Children of Israel only had a few days' journey once they left Egypt, but instead they wandered into the wilderness for 40 years.

◊ Saul was supposed to remain the King of Israel, but he was replaced by David.

◊ Esau should have inherited his father's blessing, but instead it was given to Jacob.

◊ Judas could have been one of the 12 Apostles, but instead he is known throughout history as the world's worst betrayer.

Everyone I named had a predetermined life, but somehow their actions altered those events.

How are your actions altering the events in your life?

Here is a thought...

God is in control but he allows our lives to be altered to teach us lessons. The lessons we learn while fulfilling our destiny should give us the wisdom we need to sustain our purpose.

Now, back to my original question...Are you more afraid of dying or not living your destiny?

Let me leave you with a short prayer that I have internalized and sometimes utter...

"God don't let me die without doing all that you called me to do and being all that you called me to be."

We all will die, but not everyone completely fulfills their destiny. Will you fully fulfill yours?

Chapter Twenty-Seven
How to determine a goal

"ASK AND IT WILL BE GIVEN TO YOU; SEEK AND YOU WILL
FIND; KNOCK AND THE DOOR WILL BE OPENED FOR YOU..."
Matthew 7:7

"Paralysis of analysis" or over thinking a decision occurs
often. I believe this occurs because people are not aware of
how to make effective decisions. To assist individuals, I have
included this simple but empowering section to decrease the
chances of Paralysis of Analysis.

Questions to determine your objective:

◊   Why am I going there?
◊   What do I want to achieve?
◊   Why do I want to have this chat?
◊   Why do I want to write this correspondence
     (email, text, etc.)?
◊   Why do I want to meet with this individual?
◊   Why do I want this interview?

If two or more answers to these questions are the same
then you have found your objective...

You can only have one objective and it must clear and specific...when you have it, stick to it.

Your objective is your end in view...

Once you determine your objective, get to work in making it happen.

Chapter Twenty-Eight

Value

"YOUR SELF-WORTH CAN ONLY BE MEASURED BY HOW YOU SEE YOURSELF"...

Tony Baker

One dangerous mental health disorder is anorexia nervosa. This disorder is characterized by a person severely under eating because they see themselves as being overweight when it is obvious they are not. Individuals suffering from anorexia nervosa do not value themselves and feel as if they are lacking in some manner. When a person fails to value themselves it is difficult to have any self-worth. Value is not only important in terms of personal experiences. Goods and services also carry a value that is used to determine product prices.

Little Cesar's Pizza showed the country the real value of pizza by only charging $5.

Planet Fitness showed everyone the value of gym membership by charging $10 per month.

McDonald's has a dollar menu showing us the value of food.

However, you will never see a Bentley or Rolls Royce on sale.

Why, because they cost what they cost.

These automobiles are never advertised to the major public because the people that buy them are in a different class, which is the upper class.

Today, remember your value as a person. You are also in a special class.

The Rolls Royce attracts certain kinds of people and they are still going strong. The Saturn attracted certain kinds of people and they are no longer in business.

Decide today that you are a person of value and not a cheap copy that will go out of business.

Chapter Twenty-Nine

7 Ways to Quickly Make Connections to Influence Confidants and Co-Workers

"A MAN THAT HATH FRIENDS MUST SHOW HIMSELF FRIENDLY..."

Proverbs 18:24

There is an old school rap song called, "Friends" by Whodini. The chorus line of the songs says, "Friends how many of us have them...friends the ones we can depend on...let's be friends..." Well in this section principles will be shared to help you make friends.

◊ Consciously practicing being a likeable and positive person around others will encourage others to be more open and nice as well. Most people respond well to a positive atmosphere and mindset. This is because the general mood and atmosphere tends to be lighter.

◊ Behaving in a mature yet friendly manner is also encouraged. This too is an example most people respect and admire. With admiration, there is some level of wanting to follow the example set.

◊ Always trying to be or do the best that one is capable of is also another good example to set and one that will garner certain emulation from those around.

◊ Being a good friend, especially in times of need, is an example worth setting if one expects the same treatment in return. This example not only portrays good human values, but also garners respect and admiration and maybe even encouragement for others to follow.

◊ Keeping a relaxed and nonthreatening demeanor is recommended when one is trying to set a good example. Frightening people away by being too rigid and controlling is something that should be avoided.

◊ Acknowledging one's shortcomings and flaws often helps those around with similar problems relate better and eventually be more comfortable. Setting this example also allows people to be comfortable in reaching out and generally feeling relaxed.

◊ A welcoming individual is often an individual who is never short of friends because of the example of being welcoming and nonjudgmental.

Chapter Thirty
Time, Fame, and Money

"THERE IS A TIME FOR EVERYTHING, AND A SEASON FOR EVERY ACTIVITY UNDER THE HEAVENS..."
Ecclesiastes 3:1

An argument once took place between Time, Money, and Fame.

Money said to Time and Fame,

"I am the greatest of all because with me people can buy anything they want. Money makes the world go around, so this why I am the most important."

Fame interjected and stated,

"No, no, no, it is Fame that matters the most. If you have Fame the Money will always follow...

Fame is what people seek after. They know that Money sometimes comes and goes, but for Fame people are willing to pay a price...Besides, everyone that I know wants some type of notoriety."

As Fame and Money continued to go back and forth about who is the most important, they both looked over at Time and said, "What do you have to say?" But Time said nothing.

Time stood still.

Time began to move. Fame and Money tried to stop it.

Time passed them by.

As Time passed, Fame and Money yelled, "Hey wait for us."

It yelled back and said,

"Time waits for no one."

Regardless of how much Fame and Money you have, without Time to be famous or to spend Money you are left with nothing. This is why one of man's most precious assets is Time.

Chapter Thirty-One

How to Avoid the Biggest Social Media Mistake

"BIG NUMBERS DON'T ALWAYS MEAN BIG IMPACT IN SOCIAL MEDIA"...

Tony Baker

Social media can be a very deceptive way of determining your effectiveness. It is my hope that after reading this section you become less worried about feedback and more concerned about reaching back.

To be honest with you, I have never gotten more than 30 likes on a Facebook post.

Prior to me starting a blog, I had never received a comment on anything that I posted.

Does this mean that I am not effective?

I don't believe so.

It also does not mean that the popularity of social media is not important.

There was one guy who was much like you and I. On the contrary, he may have been worse. Who was he...?

Noah.

Noah was not popular during his day.

Do you remember Noah? He and his family were the only survivors of the flood.

Noah talked about God for more than 120 years, which also includes his labor of building the Ark.

With all of that effort, not one person was convinced that Noah knew what he was talking about.

In essence, no one believed in Noah; Let me park here for a moment and ask,

"Do you sometimes feel that no one believes in you?"

Here is some news.

Any visions or dreams worth living will cause you to feel ostracized at times.

You may even feel like a failure while believing in something you have never accomplished before. Or, you may feel that God takes his time with you but rushes to make others' dreams come true (at least I do).

The interesting fact is that it had never rained on the earth before.

This may be the reason why people thought Noah was crazy. If Noah had a Facebook page in his day then the following probably would have happened:

◊ People would have ignored his friend request.
◊ Noah would have been unfriended by everyone.
◊ Every post he wrote would've received negative comments.
◊ Even worse, he would have been ignored.

The Social Media Myth That Holds People Back *is measuring your effectiveness based upon your page views on YouTube, Likes on Facebook, Tweets on Twitter, or comments on Instagram.*

Don't allow the fear of unpopularity to stop you from sharing something uplifting or informative.

If you have a unique perspective or point of view then let your voice be heard.

We know how the story ends with Noah.

My question to you is,

"How will your story end?"
Stop holding back and go for it!

"Have you ever really applied yourself and given your best effort? Imagine the possibilities."
Tony Baker

Chapter Thirty-Two

13 Surprising Principles of Achievement

"YOU MUST ALWAYS BE YOUR BIGGEST FAN AS YOU MOVE FORWARD IN YOUR FUTURE"...

Tony Baker

Success can't always be measured by more money, fancier cars, or bigger houses. I discovered more implicit ways of determining success. Grab a hold of these ideologies and apply them to your life immediately.

Have buoyant thinking

Of course, it is easier said than done. But it can be practiced. If you always look at things in a positive way, even when everything seems awry, you will always stay composed. Also, the connection between mind and body is very strong. If you are always thinking positively, it is amazing how things usually just start to fall where they should be.

Know that negative thoughts are normal

Negative thoughts are scary because they are an indication that something is very wrong. But once you learn to accept that it is only normal to feel that way, you will soon get used to it and begin to feel better. For example, it might scare you that your boss is always shouting. But once you convince yourself that shouting is his normal voice and tone, it will no longer scare you.

Be your own inspiration

The danger with having an inspiration is the possibility of falling over once the source of inspiration is gone. For example, if you are persevering with a goal because of a special someone, a breakup can make you lose your commitment to keep doing better. This is why it is important that you make yourself one of your own inspirations. No matter what, you will always be there for yourself even when everyone else is not.

Exercise humble optimism

Thinking positively will help you go a long way. But if you are always overly optimistic, you might be paving way for greater disappointment. When being optimistic, you should approach it with a humble heart. Know which goals are realistic and which are unrealistic. Always remember that optimism and positive thinking should still be based on facts and possible outcomes.

Exercise healthy pessimism

The word 'pessimism' always appears as a negative word. However, it can actually help you in your goals. Of course, you should not always think that things will go wrong. But if you somehow expect the possibility, you will not feel as disappointed or as frustrated when the failure actually takes place. You will be able to bounce back right away.

Visualize the steps you need to take

If you know which path to take, which turns to go to, and which blocks to avoid while on your journey to reaching your goals, you will feel more confident because you know what you are doing. So before starting your quest for achievement, you should visualize how you plan to get there.

Avoid becoming the perfectionist

If you are going to do it, you better do it right – or so a perfectionist would say. And yes, this is a good approach. But try not to overdo it. Nobody can be too perfect about everything and aiming for perfection will only bring you more disappointment and frustration.

Sort out the unimportant worries

We have many worries in life. However, many of them are unimportant and have nothing to do with our main goals. Sort out these less important ones, purge them, and you will have more energy to take on the problems that really matter. Taking a load off your shoulders will make you feel invigorated and revitalized. For example, if you need to do something about your grades in school or your performance at work, maybe you should first stop worrying about your lacking budget for that upcoming Disney vacation.

Have a simple eye

Having a simple eye means being satisfied with simple things and wanting simple things. This way, your own self will not be difficult to please. Also, your goals will be easier to achieve. A person with a simple approach to life is less often frustrated and disappointed. They are living lightly with fewer worries in life.

Loosen up the gear

It means you should not be too strict with yourself. So instead of telling yourself what you must do, what you need to do, and what standards to follow, why not loosen up a bit and try going easier on yourself? Many cannot see it, but the worst bully can be one's ownself. If you loosen up a bit, maybe you will start feeling lighter. And soon, you will again have the energy to get back on track.

Be honest with yourself

In other words, you should not feed yourself with lies. For example, it may be heartbreaking to admit that a business you started is already going bankrupt. If you keep lying to yourself, you are only prolonging your suffering. Instead, you should embrace the truth of the situation. That way you can have a clear mind to make the best decisions possible.

Have open expectations

Frustrations are mostly the product of expecting too much. There is truth when the proverbs said: *"An expectation postponed makes the heart sick."* So learn to expect only what is realistic and possible. And even though you are expecting a certain outcome, have an open mind that it may not happen how you expected it to be.

Do not allow gaps in your schedule

Motivation is something that needs to be fed continuously. If you are chasing a goal, make sure that you do not give it little rest until you achieve it. This is because little pauses can make you slack. With each pause, you might need to regain yourself again before restarting. This, of course, does not mean that you cannot rest. It simply means that you need to give it your all every time.

Chapter Thirty-Three

41 Empowering Proverbs

"A GOOD PROVERB IS LIKE A WARM HOUSE ON A WINTRY
DAY"...

Tony Baker

The waiting man gets the wind behind him.
Swedish Proverb

The longer the night lasts, the more our dreams will be.
Chinese Proverb

Without perseverance, talent is a barren bed.
Welsh Proverb

Failure teaches you more than success.
Russian Proverb

Nothing is impossible for a willing heart.
French Proverb

Do not be afraid of growing slowly; be afraid only of standing still.
Chinese Proverb

The first step is always the hardest.
American Proverb

If every man would sweep his own door-step the city would soon be clean.
Welsh Proverb

Many hands make light work.
English Proverb

God gives to those who get up early.
Russian Proverb

For tomorrow belongs to the people who prepare for it today.
African Proverb

Put off for one day and ten days will pass.
Korean Proverb

If at first you don't succeed, try, try again.
American Proverb

Even a stone gets rounded by constant rubbing.
Indian Proverb

Behave toward everyone as if receiving a guest.
Chinese Proverb

A man who chases two rabbits catches none.
Roman Proverb

From little acorns mighty oaks do grow.
American Proverb

If you are patient in one moment of anger, you will escape a hundred days of sorrow.
Chinese Proverb

Better one day as a lion than a hundred as a sheep.
Italian Proverb

Fall seven times, stand up eight.
Japanese Proverb

Don't set sail on someone else's star.
African Proverb

A turtle travels only when it sticks its neck out.
Korean Proverb

He who begins many things finishes but few.
Italian Proverb

One kind word can warm three winter months.
Japanese Proverb

A dose of adversity is often as needful as a dose of medicine.
American Proverb

A lie travels around the world while truth is putting her boots on.
French Proverb

A wise man changes his mind, a fool never does.
Spanish Proverb

It is not what you are called, but what you answer to.
African Proverb

Be the first to the field and the last to the couch.
Chinese Proverb

Better ask ten times than go astray once.
Yiddish Proverb

He who talks too much, errs much.
Spanish Proverb

Abundance is from activity.
Turkish Proverb

Even a fish wouldn't get into trouble if it kept its mouth shut.
Korean Proverb

A slip of the foot may soon be recovered; but that of the tongue perhaps never will.
Danish Proverb

If you want to judge a man's character, give him power.
English Proverb

Give time, time.
Italian Proverb

The truly rich are those who enjoy what they have.
Yiddish Proverb

Ten men, ten minds.
Japanese Proverb

Praise loudly, blame softly.
Russian Proverb

It is not disgraceful to ask, it is disgraceful not to ask.
Turkish Proverb

Chapter Thirty-Four
How to Engage Your Dreams

"YOU CAN'T ACHIEVE WHAT YOU HAVEN'T IDENTIFIED"...

Tony Baker

Nothing happens until something happens! In other words, you must be actively pursuing what you really desire. I teach some simple, but powerful techniques on how you can gain more grounds in terms of living the life you want.

Accomplishing a goal needs a lot of hard work, and hard work calls for infinite levels of motivation, a limitless drive to take action, discipline, making forfeitures, maintaining a favorable attitude, defeating issues, keeping one's confidence and so forth. In turn, this calls for a particular willingness and preparation fueled by inner drive and willingness to overcome enormous challenges. With that being said, here are some top flight principles to assist you in achieving and identifying your dreams.

Action–Accomplishing any goal and target calls for getting your hands dirty; that is, you have to do something and take action on the goals you've set. And you won't do anything about it unless you're motivated to do so; and you'll simply be dreaming castles in the air with nothing becoming true.

Goal arranging and designing–Are you inspired to arrange your goal and have the drive to help yourself accomplish most of what you've set out to accomplish? Are you able to arrange yet another goal and go on charging ahead towards it?

Solely specifying and setting your goal won't be enough to motivate you to carry out the necessary tasks with drive and determination; but even prior to that, you need inspiration and motivation to really specify and arrange these goals. Put simply, you require motivation right from the very beginning to get you excited about goal arranging, and having enough of it to help carry you through your jobs to finally accomplish your goals.

Discipline–Accomplishing one's goals calls for exerting discipline and stern keeping to whatever has been designed. This is only conceivable when there's sufficient self-command and drive to enforce such levels of discipline upon one's self.

Self-growth-Nobody may claim to know everything, but studying is one way to heighten your knowledge about the world. Each individual has their own limits and failings, maybe owing to the way they've been previously taught and the sort of education they've been exposed to. But when you set out to accomplish something, this learning process gets accelerated frequently and enables you to learn more and get better equipped to accomplish your goals.

This is where motivation comes in; to inspire a review and grow; to subdue all weaknesses you might have. Yes indeed, self-betterment and upgrading calls for inspirational motivation and all of this is derived from the inner drive and self-command you possess. Without motivation, most individuals won't be willing to make the sacrifice of time and work to upgrade.

Forfeiture–Are you geared up to forfeit your leisure activities and limit recreational time with your loved ones to commit to your job at hand? It's crucial that you're able to place your goal as one of your greatest priorities; over and above everything else which ought to take 2nd place.

If you're not motivated enough to be entirely dedicated to your goals, it will be practically impossible for you to make forfeitures and provide your goal that first position in your life. When you allow everything else to get in the way, your goals will be brushed aside, ignored and sooner or later forgotten.

Making any sacrifice calls for a deep sense of commitment to your personal wants, your reasons, your motives and innermost intentions; only then will you be willing, geared up and enthusiastic enough to see through your goals; without becoming tempted by additional distractions or excuses.

Remember that addressing excuses will always be your first and biggest obstacle to accomplishing your goals – so it's crucial you set your mind on what you wish and not fall prey to distractions.

"You can't live big, with small thinking."
Tony Baker

Chapter Thirty-Five

10 Ways to Identify and Deal with Stress

"WHEN ANXIETY WAS GREAT WITHIN ME, YOUR
CONSOLATION BROUGHT JOY TO MY SOUL."

Psalms 94:19 NIV

While working in an administrative capacity at a school, I experienced something quite frightening. At the time, I was under a great deal of stress. While working one day, all of sudden I got a headache. It was so severe that it brought me to my knees. I called my administrative assistant. She called my wife and I was rushed to the hospital. It turned out that my blood pressure had spiked due to stress. I was unable to identify the warning signs. Otherwise, I may have taken better precautions. Here are 10 ways to help you identify stress so that you won't find yourself in the hospital like me, or worse dead. Here is another prospective, *"Dead people don't dream."*

◊ You experience sudden anger. Have you noticed that you easily get angry and lash out at the people near you, like your partner, co-worker, friends or family members? If this is happening to you with no apparent reason, beware. You might be experiencing stress overload without you knowing it.

◊ You are feeling beaten even with small things that you do in your life. If you feel quite burdened by your normal routine and you are having that feeling of wanting to just go away and leave it all behind, you are overly stressed.

◊ You worry too much without significant reason. If you find that you are worrying too much for almost the entire day, you have reached your limit of stress.

◊ You are feeling depressed and unmotivated to work; if what interested you before doesn't interest you anymore. Or, when you don't feel excited about doing the things you used to do before for pleasure.

◊ You easily get exhausted, and despite being tired you find it hard to sleep because your mind is still thinking about so many concerns keeping you wide awake the whole night.

◊ You are suffering from constant colds and when somebody else is having colds or fevers you easily catch the virus, but your recovery is slower than usual.

◊ You find it hard to concentrate as your mental capacity is deteriorating. Your memory is also fading, which makes you forget even the thing you are doing just a while ago.

◊ You are having mood swings. From happy to being sad, to the point where you just want to burst out with tears for no reason at all.

◊ You are starting to care less about yourself, your appearance, your relationship and your environment. It doesn't matter anymore if you don't brush your hair or say I love you to your partner, like you always do.

◊ You always lack time, like some evil took half of your day.

Chapter Thirty-Six
How to Keep Your Blessings

"MAY HE GIVE YOU THE DESIRE OF YOUR HEART AND MAKE
ALL YOUR PLANS SUCCEED"...

Psalm 20:4 NIV

Moses is one of the most celebrated leaders of all time.

It is often expressed that his biggest problem was his incapability of speaking.

On the contrary, Moses' greatest challenge was not his inability to communicate but his self-limiting belief.

Outside of speaking, God showed him several strengths he possessed as well as introduced him to a new level of personal power.

He was shown how a stick can become a snake and how he could alter the pigmentation of his hand. He was even given power over the natural resource of water through his staff.

In spite of God's confirmation and encouragement, Moses still refused to believe in himself. I feel that most people are like Moses.

They have tremendous talent but they are tainted with a bottom line self-belief. It was Moses' lack of self-confidence that hindered his flow.

God wanted to bless Moses in a greater dimension. He wanted to empower him to communicate his message to free the Children of Israel from one of the most powerful men on earth; The Pharaoh of Egypt.

Instead of allowing his blessings to flow, he forfeited them due to fear. God eventually chose Moses' brother Aaron as the spokesman.

Remember, whenever you are given a new challenge at least give it a try. God is on your side and He wants you to keep your blessings flowing.

Chapter Thirty-Seven
Principles of Time Management

"UNMANAGED TIME ONLY PRODUCES EXCUSES AND NOT OUTCOMES"...

Tony Baker

We all have said it, "Man where did the time go?" This happens sometimes when we have wasted precious moments on activities that don't yield any results. One of the keys to achieving your objectives is learning time management skills. Therefore, I have included this section to assist you. The first section provides basic Time Management Skills. The second section deals with Time Management for study skills. Time Management for a balanced life is listed last.

Time Management Skills
- ◊ List down all your activities.
- ◊ Determine the positive and the negative time spending practice.
- ◊ Keep a log on how long you normally do your activities such as homework, exam and tests

preparation, extra-curricular activities and more.

◊ Plan and create a schedule based on your real time record.

◊ Do your task on time as noted and do it once. There is no point in doing the same things twice, like listening to a recorded lecture or rewriting a messy note.

◊ Master the art of concentration. You can be more productive if you focus on one task at a time. For instance, focus more on the lessons and not on small talks. If your brain is trained to concentrate on learning and listening for a span of 15 minutes, reprogram your brain to pay attention even further.

Time Management for studying

◊ Determine what is more important and make a list according to the level of importance.

◊ Create an achievable weekly to-do list. This can help you fill in vacant time while you are waiting for your next class or school activity. Look for a study place where you are most comfortable studying. Your room should be out of the options as it is more conducive for sleeping and relaxing rather than learning.

◊ In school, reading assignments are sometimes overflowing. You have to have a strategy to adjust and skim all of your materials.

◊ Avoid group studies. Research shows that studying alone or with a single study partner is more efficient than studying in a large group.

Time Management for balancing your life

◊ Learn and practice how to be organized. Having everything in order will let you do things easily and stress free, which will help you save significant time for other valuable tasks.

◊ When you plan out your to-do list and set your schedules, allocate 10 to 15 minutes allowance for yourself to prepare for the next task.

◊ Be realistic when making your action plan and schedules. You may want to first observe your activities and time spending habits before you go ahead and make a plan.

◊ Make your fixed schedules known to your direct supervisor, clients, classmates, friends and family; so that they will not distract you on those times.

◊ Working and at the same time studying in school is definitely draining. However, you can manage your stress if you have proper time management skills.

"If today was your last day on earth would you be happy with your results?"
Tony Baker

Chapter Thirty-Eight

God As We Know Him

A PRIEST SAID "I PRAYED ABOUT MY DREAMS." A BUDDHIST SAID "I MEDITATED ABOUT MY DREAMS." A MUSLIM SAID, "I FASTED ABOUT MY DREAMS." A CATHOLIC SAID, "I WENT TO EUCHARIST ABOUT MY DREAMS." A CHRISTIAN SAID, "I TALKED WITH JESUS ABOUT MY DREAMS." IF THEY ONLY DID THIS TELL ME WHICH WILL EVER LIVE THEIR DREAMS...

Tony Baker

"MORE THAN 9 IN 10 (OR 92% OF) AMERICANS STILL SAY "YES" WHEN ASKED THE BASIC QUESTION "DO YOU BELIEVE IN GOD?"

Gallup Poll

Perhaps you are in the minority and do not believe in God. Surprisingly, the majority of Americans believe otherwise. This means that you should consider a higher power. My higher power is Jesus Christ of the Bible. However, this section is not about you accepting my belief system, but more about you establishing one.

In my opinion a personal faith is very important. I know you may believe in your mother, grandmother, or other relatives and friends. Throughout the years I have learned that people will fail you. Some of the most important people in my life have failed me. As much as I love my wife, I must admit that she has failed me and likewise I have failed her.

The truth of the matter is this. Your faith in God gives you support from a person that knows more about you than you do about yourself. God as you know Him has a great plan for your life. He desires to fellowship with you through rough times. God also desires to encourage you when you feel like a failure. He longs to be your friend when others have forsaken you.

In conclusion, I would encourage you to direct or redirect your effort to get a relationship with God. Think of it this way, if you believe in God then what do you have to lose? You have not lost any money, sleep, or clothing. The truth of the matter is that you will only benefit if you trust God. Furthermore, if you don't believe in God, He believes in you. Have a little faith!

www.ingramcontent.com/pod-product-compliance
Lightning Source LLC
Chambersburg PA
CBHW071819020426
42331CB00007B/1539